Built Like That

by Jan Anderson

PM Plus Non Fiction

Sapphire

U.S. Edition © 2013 HMH Supplemental Publishers
10801 N. MoPac Expressway
Building #3
Austin, TX 78759
www.hmhsupplemental.com

Text © 2003 Cengage Learning Australia Pty Limited
Illustrations © 2003 Cengage Learning Australia Pty Limited
Originally published in Australia by Cengage Learning Australia

5 6 7 8 9 10   1957   16 15 14 13
4500398487

Text: Jan Anderson
Printed in China by 1010 Printing International Ltd

Acknowledgments

Photographs by The Australian Greenhouse Office, p. 18; Australian Picture Library/ Corbis/ ART on FILE, pp. 29 top, 29 bottom/ Andrew Brown, p. 8 bottom/ Micael Busselle, p. 31 right/ Owen Franken,
p. 4 left/ Gaetano, p. 7 bottom right, Dallas & John Heaton, p. 9/ Bill Miles, p. 7 top left/ Greg Nikas, p. 7 top right/ Underwood & Underwood, p. 22 left/ Bill Varie, p. 11 bottom; Getty Images/ Stone, p. 11 top; Image Addict, p.13 centre left; Imagen/ Bill Thomas, pp. 8 top, 10, 12 top, 16, 19, 25 top; Mammoet Holdings B.V., Schiedam, the Netherlands, p. 17 top; Mary Evans Picture Library, p. 27 right; Photolibrary.com/ Index Stock Imagery, front cover top, front cover bottom left, pp. 4 right, 26 bottom, 30/ Robin Smith, front cover bottom right, p. 12 bottom/ Superstock, pp. 1, 26 top; Skyscrapers.com,
p. 17 bottom; State Library of NSW, p. 28 top; Stock Photos, pp. 5, 7 bottom left, 13 top left, 13 top right, 13 bottom right, 14, 15, 22 left, 22 right, 24, 25 bottom, 27 left, 28 bottom, 31 left/ Masterfile/ Lloyd Sutton, p. 6 right/ Stock Works, p. 6 left;

Built Like That

ISBN 978 0 75 786954 9

Contents

Introduction

This is the story of building, and how modern technology and materials make construction an interesting part of everyday life.

Many kinds of workers, from architects to plumbers, help to put up buildings. They use concrete-mixer trucks, cranes and computers, and work with materials as different from each other as glass and steel.

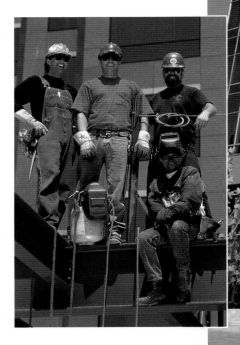

It took just a few months for this deep hole in the ground (left) to be transformed into the multi-story building (right).

Chapter 1

Who Makes It Happen?

Workers with many different kinds of training help to make a building, even a small house.

The architect designs the building and draws the plans. The builder uses these plans to decide the materials needed, what they'll cost, and how to put them together.

Did you know?

Architects use special computer programs for drawing three-dimensional pictures of a building.

Engineers test the soil so that architects can design the right foundations. Engineers also design the steel frames of tall buildings, and the concrete floors inside them.

Carpenters cut and join the timber parts of a building, like the frame.

Plumbers lay water pipes and make drains.

Roofers lay the roof tiles.

Electricians connect the power to the building, and install the wires that carry the electricity around inside. They put in light switches and outlets.

Chapter 2

Building Materials

The first houses were made of natural materials such as wood, or mud, clay, and stones. In some parts of the world, these materials are still used.

Many centuries later, people learned how to saw trees into planks, and cut rock into slates. This meant that natural materials could be put together in new, and more effective, ways.

*The roof of this house is covered in **shingles** sawn from large pieces of wood.*

An old way of **insulating** houses was to cover the roof with turf. Turf consists of pieces of grass and soil cut out of the ground. Today we would consider this to be an **eco-friendly** way of insulating, because it uses a natural material from a renewable resource.

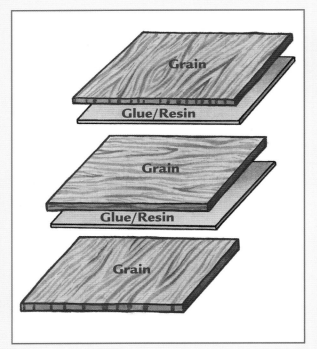

Plywood is strong because the **grain** on one sheet of wood is at right angles to the grain on the sheets next to it. Plywood is still popular today.

Over the years, many new kinds of building materials have been developed using new technology.

Some of these materials have been made by processing natural materials, like wood.

Plywood was one of the first new materials. It was invented during the 1930s. Plywood consists of thin sheets of wood that have been glued together. It is very strong.

Particleboard is made from small pieces of waste wood, like wood chips or wood fibers. These "particles" are set in **resin** to make board. Plywood and particleboard are good materials for covering walls and floors. They are quick to put in place, which saves money.

Particleboard is often used in flooring.

Did you know?
Some boards have a plastic surface. They are good for building cupboards and counter-tops in kitchens.

Metals, like **steel** and **aluminum**, are now used instead of timber for many building parts. Sheets of steel can replace tiles for roofs.

Aluminum frames for windows are replacing wooden ones. They last longer and they come in a range of colors.

The steel used on this roof has a special coating that stops it from rusting.

These houses have both window and door frames made of aluminum.

The siding on houses can be made of many different things, including wood, vinyl, aluminum, and bricks. Insulation is often used between the frame of the house and the siding to keep the house cool in summer and warm in winter.

Composites are one of the newest developments in building materials. They are made by combining two materials to make a new material.

The walls of this building are made from a composite material. It consists of plastic that has been "sandwiched" between two sheets of steel. This material is strong and wears well. The plastic layer provides good insulation.

Holding Buildings Together

Building parts must be held together firmly, or the building will break apart in the first storm or strong wind. Builders use nails, nuts and bolts, glue, screws, and even staples. Buildings with steel frames are welded together. Bricks are held together with mortar.

5000 years ago

Egyptians made nails by hand and used glue (made from some parts of animals) for joining pieces of wood.

1550

In 1550, nuts and bolts were first made in France. (They are tightened with a wrench.)

1760

In 1760, metal screws were invented for joining pieces of wood.

1903

Fouch and Picard, in France, invented **welding**, for joining pieces of metal together, such as the steel frames of some buildings.

Prefabrication

When a building is prefabricated, all or parts of it are made somewhere else. The parts are carried to the building **site**, where they are **assembled**.

The first prefabricated houses were made of wood, over 150 years ago.

This prefabricated house was built in 1839.

Did you know?
Some prefabricated houses were called "portable houses" because they could be moved.

PORTABLE HOUSES SITE
399 COVENTRY STREET, SOUTH MELBOURNE

OPEN: WEEKENDS... 1st and 3rd Sundays each month from 1pm to 4pm (Except 3rd Sunday in December and 1st in January)

THIS SUNDAY WEEKDAYS, by appointment, special openings during Summer months, School holidays... Phone 684 4771

These prefabricated cottages were very small and very hot inside in summer.

   In the next era of prefabrication, which began around 1850, iron and steel were used for the walls of prefabricated houses.

   Some prefabricated houses, like the one above, had walls made of corrugated iron. The walls, and other house parts, were cut to size in one country and transported to another, where they were assembled.

Prefabrication is becoming popular once again. It is a quick and easy way of building. It often costs less, particularly now that many building parts can be prefabricated in factories, using machines. Almost any part of a building can be prefabricated, from metal window frames to the wooden frames of roofs.

New technology has made it possible to prefabricate walls using concrete. The walls are formed in **molds**, in a factory. They have holes for the windows and doors. After the walls are made, they are carried on a big truck to the building site, where they are tilted up into place. They are then bolted together.

This kind of building is called "tilt-up." Tilt-up is a quick and easy way of building.

Did you know?
In the future, building sites might become places where a handful of workers take just days to put up a house made from prefabricated parts. At the moment, many people work for weeks or months to build a house.

This whole ten-story building was prefabricated. It was built in one city and floated on a pontoon down-river to another. It is located on the River Nieuwe in the Netherlands.

Chapter 5

Eco-friendly Building

In the future, more houses will be designed so that they are friendly to the environment. They will be built to use energy and water efficiently. They will be made from materials that can be recycled, or that have been made using the smallest amount of energy possible. In some cases, houses will be designed so that they can be pulled apart and put up again in another place. In other words, the whole house can be recycled.

Features of an eco-friendly house

- Tanks to collect the rain water that falls on the roof.
- A system to clean waste water from the kitchen and laundry, for re-use on the garden.
- **Eaves** to let in the most sun during winter, but the least sun in summer. This reduces the need for air-conditioning and heating.

- Insulation in the roof and walls.
- It is made of materials that can be recycled. The amount of energy used to make the materials, and to recycle them, will also be considered.
- A **solar** hot-water system on the roof.

This university building won an award for **sustainable** architecture.

19

"Intelligent" Houses

Chapter 6

Imagine a house that almost thinks for you!

In the future, many houses will have a computer through which you control almost everything inside. You will tell this computer what to do and when to do it, using another computer (your lap-top computer), or your mobile phone.

This means that you will be able to start up heating systems and lighting in the house from across the town, or the other side of the world. When you get home from work or vacation, the garden will be watered, the lights turned on, and the dinner cooked. Anything at home that runs on electricity, and has a mini-computer inside, will be controllable.

1. *The touch screen on the computer enables the owner to control anything in the house when they are at home as well.*
2. *Lights can be switched on.*
3. *Washing machine cycle can be changed.*
4. *Dishwasher can be started.*
5. *Video recorder can be set.*
6. *Temperature of the air-conditioning unit can be changed.*
7. *Burglar alarm can be switched on if it wasn't set before leaving home.*
8. *Garden sprinklers can be started.*

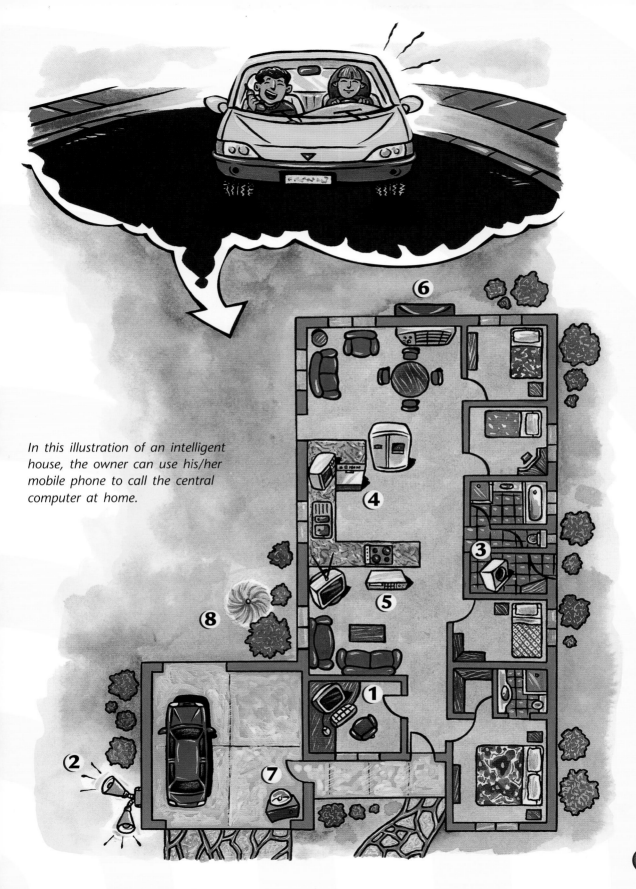

In this illustration of an intelligent house, the owner can use his/her mobile phone to call the central computer at home.

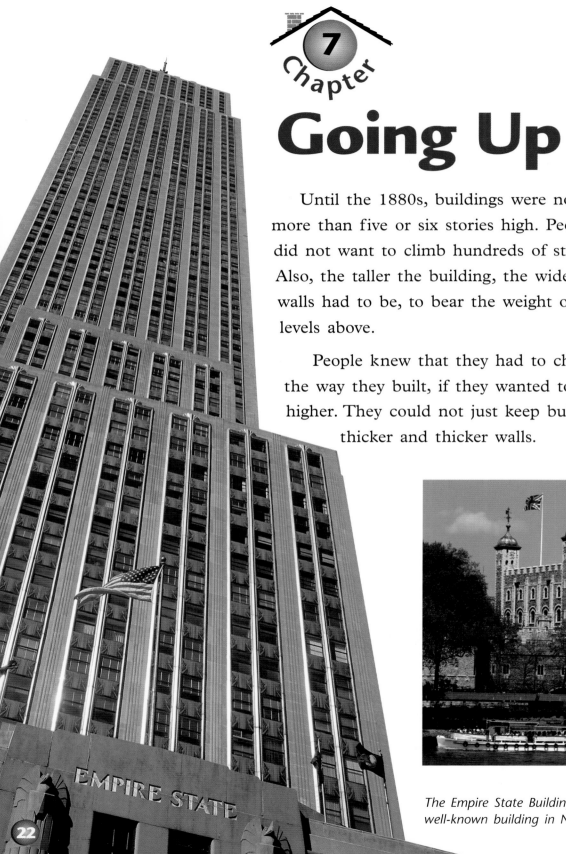

Chapter 7

Going Up . . .

Until the 1880s, buildings were no more than five or six stories high. People did not want to climb hundreds of stairs. Also, the taller the building, the wider the walls had to be, to bear the weight of the levels above.

People knew that they had to change the way they built, if they wanted to go higher. They could not just keep building thicker and thicker walls.

The Empire State Building is a well-known building in New York.

Strong steel became available during the 19th century, and this was used to make frames for very tall buildings. A new way of building was invented! The walls were hung on the frame, which carried the weight of the walls and the floors.

The development of power stations in 1882 made electricity available for lighting. The first electric elevator was designed in 1889, so people could be carried to the tops of buildings.

Electric light, and the invention of air-conditioning in 1902, meant that buildings could be deeper, and have rooms far away from windows — because natural light and **ventilation** were no longer essential.

The central part of the Tower of London is only four stories high, but the walls at ground level are almost 14 feet thick to bear the weight of the building above.

The ten-story Home Insurance Building in Chicago, IL, was the first skyscraper. It was built in 1885.

Welding

The steel frame of a tall building has to be very strong. Its parts must be joined together well. That's why they are welded.

In welding, two pieces of metal are heated until they become soft. Then they are pushed together and left to cool. A solid joint is made.

Strong welds were needed on the sliding roof of this building so that when it is pushed open or shut, it does not break apart.

When framing big buildings, teams of welders work non-stop for days. They cannot let the steel parts being joined go cold, because the joint will not be strong enough.

Building Machinery

An excavator is handy because it can do two jobs. It has a bucket with sharp teeth for digging trenches (for foundations and laying water pipes). It can also level the ground with its shovel.

With the invention of big machines, such as concrete-mixer trucks and cranes, building has become easier. Without them, it would have been impossible to construct many of the high-rise buildings we see in our cities today.

Bulldozers are used to clear trees on building sites, and to level the ground ready for building.

The shovel has a sharp blade for cutting into the ground and through tree trunks. It scoops up the dirt and dumps it into trucks that carry it away.

Metal tracks make it easy to move over bumpy ground, and grip soft, wet earth.

Cranes are used for lifting heavy materials on a building site. There are several kinds of cranes.

This crane is called a tower crane.
It can extend upward as a building gets higher. It has a counterweight
at one end to balance the load being lifted which stops the crane from toppling over.

Did you know?

Workers on a building site must wear protective clothing, like hard hats and steel-capped boots. Their colored vests make them visible to other workers, who are operating machines like cranes.

This is an old-style concrete mixer. Modern models have a motor to turn the mixer.

Before concrete factories and concrete-mixer trucks were developed, workers had to mix concrete by hand on the building site. It was hard, slow work, as the concrete could only be made in small amounts.

As the concrete-mixer truck travels to the building site, the drum on the back turns so that the concrete, which is like a paste, does not set. At the site, the truck pumps the concrete down a chute at the back, or through a long hose.

Concrete is being pumped from the truck up to the top story of the building.

Famous Buildings

During the 20th century, new technology enabled people to build some amazing buildings.

The Sydney Opera House in Australia looks as though it will drift into Sydney Harbor, with its sail-like roof of concrete and shimmering white tiles. Completed in 1973, some people call this magnificent building the "eighth wonder of the world."

The segments of each shell were made of concrete. The concrete was cast in molds of the right shapes, on the building site. The segments were then lifted into place using huge tower cranes. Strong **cables**, made of steel, were used to join the concrete segments together.

The Sydney Opera House

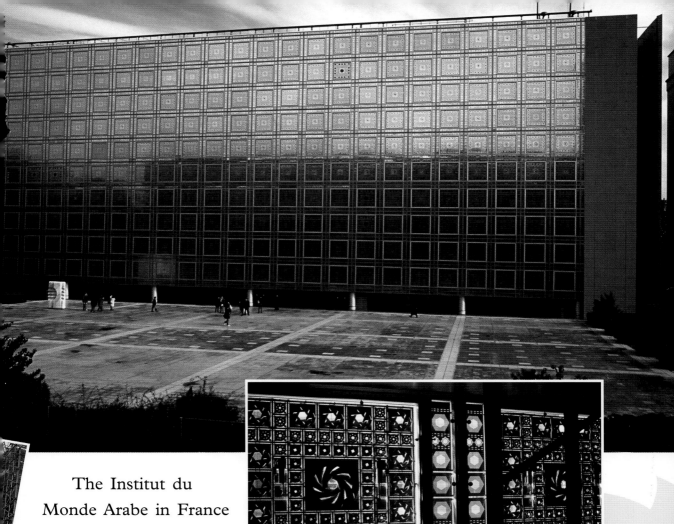

The Institut du Monde Arabe in France is famous not only for its beautiful architecture, but also for its interesting windows.

On the side that faces the sun, the windows have metal screens that sense how much light is entering the building. These screens then adjust to let in more, or less, light — depending on how sunny it is.

The Transamerica Pyramid was designed to be safe in an earthquake. It is in San Francisco, California.

Between the ground floor and the fifth floor, there are 20 pyramids of steel that help keep this part of the building rigid in an earthquake. The upper floors have been designed to **flex** a little, rather than break when the ground moves. The Transamerica Pyramid has already been "tested" in an earthquake, in 1989. It swayed around, but it survived well.

Did you know?
The triangular pyramid is one of the strongest shapes.

The Pompidou Centre in Paris, France is an art museum. When it was built, some people thought it looked "inside out!" All the pipes for carrying water, electricity, heat and air-conditioning are on the outside, instead of the inside.

The pipes are color-coded: green for water and white for ventilation ducts.

The escalators are also on the outside and provide a wonderful view of the city.

Glossary

aluminum	a very light metal
assembled	put together
cables	metal wires
composites	materials made by combining different materials
eaves	the overhanging edges of a roof
eco-friendly	kind to the environment
flex	to bend
grain	the pattern of lines on wood
insulating (insulation)	stopping heat or cold getting in or out of a house
mold	a container used to form a particular shape
resin	a type of glue
shingles	thin pieces of wood or slate used as roof tiles
site	the place where a building will be built
solar	from the sun
steel	a strong metal made from iron
sustainable	building that is done without harming the environment
ventilation	the free movement of air
welding	heating two pieces of metal to join them together